CHO[illegible]
INFERNAL

By
REG FRARY

With illustrations by
Madeleine R. Parker

NORHEIMSUND BOOKS AND CARDS
1 Whitney Road,
Burton Latimer,
Kettering
Northamptonshire
NN15 5SL

First published in 1994

By the same author
DON'T UPSET THE CHOIR
WHAT ABOUT THE CHOIR, VICAR?
HAVE YOU HEARD OUR CHOIR?
DON'T BLAME THE ORGANIST

ISBN 0 948852 43 7

Printed by Peter Dawes Printers
6 Canon Street, Kettering, Northamptonshire
Tel: (0536) 85524 Fax: (0536) 412032

DEDICATION

Remembering all the charming choir girls who appear in my stories - and a flautist in a certain Salzburgerland brass band who I'd love to include in them if only she were a choir girl too.

CHOIRS INFERNAL

PREFERABLY A PHILISTINE

"I hope he won't be a genius. Geniuses can be quite a nuisance".

"Or a moron - morons can be awkward, too".

"Or a relation of the vicar. Fancy having another one like him".

"Or a philistine".

"I don't know about a philistine. Perhaps a philistine would be best for us. You know how the vicar likes to call us philistines because we're always singing old favourites and won't do anything new".

"Yes, I reckon you're right. Let's look out for a philistine".

The discussion was taking place among members of a West country parish church choir in the vestry after Sunday Evensong. As a not infrequent visitor in the choir and an old friend of one or two of the senior members, I was a privileged onlooker.

Things were getting unusually exciting for the choir these days. A new organist and choirmaster was in the process of being chosen - the previous one having decided that his destiny lay in playing tea-time piano music on a cruise liner - and a short list of three applicants had been agreed upon. The idea was that each should be allotted a weekend during which he would conduct the Friday night choir practice and play at the three Sunday services, thus giving the choir the opportunity to make their choice of a leader. The first of the three was to take charge of the choir during the following weekend...

"A full house", beamed the vicar, as he surveyed the crowded choirstalls on Friday evening. "Splendid! Splendid! And to conduct the practice tonight I have the pleasure - indeed, very *great* pleasure - in introducing -" and he went on - and on - about the small, apparently multi - talented young man at his side, who kept on rising on the balls of his feet and seemed to be critically appraising the chancel ceiling. Eventually, at a loss for any more words of praise, the vicar reluctantly stopped and stepped back.

"the small apparently multi-talented young man at his side"

The young man stood before us and I had the most forceful feeling that he would have appreciated it if we'd all jumped to attention and saluted. We didn't , of course, and, having lowered his eyes to regard with silent distaste half a house-brick that was supporting the end of the battered choirstall at his side, he looked us over with an expression that could have been one of puzzlement or contempt or both. "I suppose you *can* all read music?" he said, letting his eyes drift to the ceiling again. There were mumbles and grunts in reply, but no definite confirmation that some of us could read music, or admission that most of us couldn't and had to rely on the choirmaster bashing out the tune over and over again on the vestry piano until we knew it by heart. The young man picked up a psalter."I don't like the pointing in this psalter", he announced. "I want you to sing a few verses of psalm 67 until I can stand it no longer. Then I'll show you how to alter the pointing so that the words make some sense".

We'd only got as far as the second verse when he stopped us with a pained expression and frantic, flapping hands. "*This* is how it should be sung", he announced, and proceeded to sing the whole psalm through in a thin, wailing tenor that moved the vicar, standing next to me, to breathe: "Beautiful, oh, beautiful. "And for the rest of the practice the choir didn't have much to do at all except listen to the young man warble through all the canticles, psalms and hymns for the Sunday services, doubtless so that we should realize how much beauty we had missed in all the years before his arrival. The final item of the practice was the Evensong anthem, which members of the choir had specially chosen. It was a regularly bawled old favourite by Barnby, and it so upset the young man that he couldn't even contemplate rehearsing it. So he replaced it with something by Tallis which no one knew, but it didn't matter because the young man was more than ready to sing the solo parts to us, which immediately restored his composure and sent the vicar into ecstasies of delight.

Needless to say, the choir didn't choose this particular genius for the post of organist and choirmaster. But neither did they later endorse either of the other applicants. One was an iron-faced, cynical-eyed gentleman who looked like a retired schoolmaster of the old school, whose main aim at the practice seemed to be to make each member of the choir sing a scale solo three or four times while he made continuous little tut-tutting sounds and breathed hard. And when at last we did get the chance to sing together, he punctuated our efforts with observations like: "We are not putting just that little bit *extra* into it, are we?" and "We must learn to watch our conductor, musn't we?" and "We musn't forget what we've been told just two little minutes ago, must we?"

The other applicant, a nervous, worried-looking young man, didn't seem to have his heart in the proceedings at all. Either he'd just had a row with his girlfriend, who was sitting in the front pew with a very unfriendly expression on her face, or he didn't like the sound of the organ or the vicar. He certainly didn't like the sound of the choir and seemed to be talking to himself through most of the practice. A choir girl who was standing nearest him reckoned that he was making rude remarks about our vocal abilities. Be that as it may, he finished the practice in no time at all and was promptly marched away by the unfriendly-looking girlfriend. So neither he nor the iron-faced cynic got the job and we still had no choirmaster in sight.

Some time later I was again at the church, on this occasion helping out at a Saturday wedding service for which it had proved difficult to muster an adequate choir at short notice. For weeks, in the absence of a regular organist, a series of well-meaning members of the congregation had tried their hands at the organ ("Well, I can knock out a tune on the piano - the organ is much the same as the piano, isn't it?") but that brutish instrument stood in its dark, cobwebby corner getting more and more surly and unco-operative as it awaited someone who would really understand it and deal sympathetically with its decades-old eccentricities. Things were getting desperate, and even the vicar had expressed the view that, although he would prefer a genius for the post, he wouldn't say no to a good reliable philistine.

Luckily no volunteer organist was needed for this wedding. The bride was supplying her own, a favourite uncle who used to play a cinema organ in the great days when cinemas were like magic palaces and not like someone's living room with a screen between the window curtains. Presently he presented himself in the vestry, a beaming, rotund little man in baggy morning dress, rather self-consciously hanging on to a grey top hat. The vicar introduced him to us and we gathered round him as he went through the list of wedding music which appeared to be scribbled on the back of a bill from a local off-license. He poked a stubby finger at the scrawl."There you are, you see. She's coming in with Wagner - you know, 'Here comes the bride' - and going out with Mendelssohn. None of this new fangled stuff. And ",his finger prodding again, "the *old* tune to this hymn *and* the other two. You can't beat the old and tried stuff. Some of these parsons and organists today try to slip in all kinds of odd stuff - modern rubbish. "You have to watch 'em like a hawk". He bustled off to the organ. We remained in a circle, looking at each other, as a single exciting thought crystallized between us. Our tenor soloist voiced it. "A philistine!" he exclaimed. "A *real* philistine! Do you think he'd like a regular job?"

The wedding service went off splendidly. Everyone in the choir knew every note of the music - had known it since childhood - and they all sang merrily if not melodiously. The organ seemed to sense that it had found an understanding friend and it's sound was happy...

After the service the little organist was obviously delighted with our suggestion that he should consider the post of permanent organist and choirmaster. "Often thought I'd like to tackle a church organ", he admitted, "but never did anything about it, Y'see, it's the choirboys. Never married. Had no kids. Don't understand 'em. Wouldn't know how to keep choirboys in order. Not a clue, y'see".

Reluctantly, some of us saw him off to the wedding reception and I returned to the vestry for a coat I'd forgotten. One of our sopranos was there putting away the music. She was a beautiful girl and wholly charming and, it transpired, had just hurled a choirboy head first through the vestry doorway into the churchyard rubbish tip. He was always referred to by his mother as "our super little kid" and for months had enjoyed nothing better after a service than skateboarding round the vestry at breakneck speed and laughing so joyously and heartwarmingly at the resulting chaos and surge of unecclesiastical language.

When some of my choir colleagues heard about the choirboy-hurling incident, they went to the vicar with a suggestion and the vicar got in touch with the philistine with the same suggestion. Now the philistine is happily installed as organist and choirmaster and he doesn't have to worry overmuch about discipline among the choirboys. He has a delightful deputy who manages that side of things very ably.

THE EYE OF THE BEHOLDER

The new vicar in the village where my old woodwork master, Hacksaw, is organist is very proud of the village church. He says it's unique and full of character and keeps on photographing it and getting artists to draw bits of it.

It looks like an eighteenth-century folly. It wasn't built as a folly, of course, but throughout the eighteenth and nineteenth centuries enormously rich and generous patrons and devil-may-care local builders with widely differing artistic tastes or no taste at all had the time of their lives adding turrets and bits of thatching and fat stone cherubs all over the place, and knocking out peerless Norman doorways and mediaeval windows to accommodate an outsize memorial chapel with a music hall ceiling and a hefty castellated West porch reminiscent of the entrance to a Victorian railway tunnel.

The new vicar's admiration knows no bounds.

He likes the choir too, he reckons that never anywhere has he come across a choir even remotely like Hacksaw's. He says they've got that elusive something which is indescribable.

On a recent fine Sunday morning when I was in the vicinity, and arrived early to sing in Hacksaw's choir, a glamourous choir girl (Hacksaw always has glamourous choir girls in his choir because he says that, stuck up there in the chancel in full view of everybody, the choir should at least *look* attractive even if they can't sing attractively) was conducting a tweed-clad, elderly, peering man with a notebook around the outside of the church and beaming at him and everything in general. I joined them.

"What *period* is the church?" asked the man, with a slightly puzzled air.

"Period?" repeated the choir girl. "It's all periods. We've got the lot here". She pointed to the parapet. "You see all those little knobs and things along the top? They were put up for Queen Victoria's Diamond Jubilee".

"Restoration", shuddered the peering man.

"I expect so", ran on the choir girl. "And this big bit stuck on the side here is a memorial chapel for the people who used to live in the big house on the green. They've all gone now, and it's a sort of borstal". The peering man seemed to be having difficulty in looking at the memorial chapel.

"The tower's really old", his guide went on. "It was here when my grandad was a boy".

"It's fifteenth century", said the man.

"Yes, quite likely", agreed the choir girl. "It hasn't got any electric light. The bellringers have to use oil lamps".

"Strange!" Her charge was craning his neck sideways. "There's a thatched roof round the back here."

"That's our choir vestry", said the girl. "It used to have a tin roof, and a slice of the tin fell off one Sunday evening - they say Hacksaw was going mad on the organ with a bit of Wagner - he gets out of control with Wagner sometimes - makes the whole place shake - and this slice of tin nearly brained the churchwarden's cat so someone gave the money to thatch it - the roof, that is, not the cat", she clarified, and her smile was irresistible.

"Extraordinary!" murmured the peering man, mesmerized. Slowly he shifted a glazed gaze to a memorial plaque on the wall. "Late eighteenth century", he wavered. "Very nice". The choir girl nodded at the flamboyant wording that commended the deceased. "He used to play a viol in the gallery before we had an organ", she explained. "There's a lot about him in the history of the parish my Uncle Ted wrote. You can get it for 10p at the back of the church. The choir used to sit in the gallery in those days. I wouldn't like to do that. They had to sit on planks of wood with no backs". He still peered at the plaque. "I like all those cherubs crawling round it", said the choir girl. "Jolly fat, though, aren't they? If people had babies as fat as that now, they'd be no end worried".

The peering man looked up at the East window, and his voice warmed. "Again, fifteenth century", he almost purred. "Beautiful fifteenth century".

"Yes", agreed the choir girl. "Funny, too. On sunny summer mornings the sun shines through it right on to the choir and all our faces look green and red".

The peering man gazed at her. "A beautiful, beautiful window. Think of it! - put here over five hundred years ago".

"Yes", said the choir girl, "and this is the vestry door. My brother - he's a carpenter - fixed it last Saturday. The old one had fallen to bits. Looks a bit new for around here, but it'll blend in better when he stains it".

Just then the door in question opened and an agitated Hacksaw looked out. He ignored the peering man, greeted me fleetingly and urgently appealed to the choir girl. "I can't find the anthem copies for 'Hear my Prayer'", he announced.

"Where's Jack?" asked the choir girl. "He's got lots of places where he keeps things - oh, of course, he's on holiday".
"I've looked everywhere", said Hacksaw.
"Have you looked under the radiator behind the organ?" asked the choir girl. "There's an old shoe box - or in the broom cupboard? There's lots of junk in there".
"The broom cupboard - ah!" Hacksaw bounced off and in a few moments was back with a wad of yellowing, tattered music. "Good for you", he said. "Good old 'Hear my prayer'".
"You mean we're doing it this morning?" asked the choir girl. "We haven't practiced it".
"Yes, we have - when we did it last time", said Hacksaw.
"That was two years ago", reminded the choir girl. "Who's singing the solo?"
"You are", said Hacksaw. "You'll look good singing that".
"What about if I don't know it?" suggested the choir girl.
"You'll *know* it", countered Hacksaw. "You've been in the choir long enough to tackle that without much bother. We'd better just run through it quickly before people start coming into church. We can't be kicking up a row while people are having their quiet time before the service".
"Quiet time?" repeated the choir girl. "They don't have a quiet time. They stand around gassing till they see the choir coming in, then they all rush for their pews. Anyway, why are we doing 'Hear my prayer' in such a hurry?"
Hacksaw mentioned the name of a prominent and wealthy lady who lived in a local Victorian pile called The Towers and who was eagerly supporting the vicar's latest pet projects for the parish both financially and by the frequent loan of her grounds and luxury marquee. "She has a sister

who is visiting her unexpectedly from the States", he explained, "and this sister simply adores 'Hear my prayer'. And she's coming to Matins this morning".
"I hope we don't break down", said the choir girl.
"Oh, we'll manage", assured Hacksaw comfortably. "We always do. Look at the time we did that special request Hallelujah Chorus for that wedding when more than half of us were away on holiday".
"We only had six in the choir", remembered the choir girl, "and one of those had forgotten his glasses and couldn't see the music.".
"There you are, then", said Hacksaw. "Those wedding people were no end pleased. In any case", he concluded, "from what I hear of the sister, she's not likely to notice any little slip-ups. She's not all that musical. She just thinks Mendelssohn is so romantic because he died young".
Suddenly, joyously, the bells pealed forth, drowning out Hacksaw's further words.
"That's done it", shouted the choir girl. "Now we can't even practice it".
No one ever interfered with the doings of the bellringers because they'd been there for ever. No one really knew much about them. In fact, it was a job to tell them apart. They were all rotund of figure, wore black suits with gold watch chains and bowler hats and, when not ringing, always seemed to be keeping themselves to themselves round their own special table at the back of the bar in the Black Dog.
"We'll manage", mouthed Hacksaw, and he beamed affectionately at the glamourous choir girl.
And, true to form, the choir (turning up in the revered traditional manner two minutes before the service and

having the anthem thrust into their hands as they scrambled into their robes) did manage the Mendelssohn very well and the glamourous choir girl sang like an angel. After the service the sister from The States hugged her with tears in her eyes and the vicar felt sure that now, at the vaguest suggestion from him, the parish Christmas dinner and dance could be transferred from the parish hall to the ballroom of The Towers.

"they scrambled into their robes"

As I left the vestry in company with Hacksaw and the choir girl, the peering man suddenly materialized round a corner, waving his notebook violently. "Absolutely

disgraceful!" he addressed his recent guide. "So many awful things have been done to this church. Restoration, it's called. I call it vandalism. Look at what they did to the lovely chancel. Those awful Victorian choirstalls cluttering it up and destroying its perfect proportions. What a wicked shame. They should be swept away".
"Swept away?" gasped the choir girl. "They're where the choir sit - and, proportions or no proportions, we're not going back to sitting in the gallery on planks of wood with no backs".
"Surely a small price to pay to enable your congregation to appreciate real beauty?" said the peering man.
"But the congregation couldn't *see* the choir girls if they were stuck back in the gallery", put in Hacksaw. And his face was a perfect picture of puzzlement.

THE POACHERS

At the picture-postcard village church (partly thatched, partly falling down) where my friend Oscar is a long-term chorister, relations between the vicar and the choir couldn't be more harmonious. The vicar never interferes with the music, leaving the choice of hymns and settings for the services entirely to the choir who leave it entirely to the organist who sticks faithfully to a list handed down from the last organist but one. The choir and organist greatly appreciate the vicar's attitude and, in return, always keep the sound of their homely chatter during the sermon down to a reasonable hum, and immediately and wholeheartedly respond to the vicar's well-known winter appeals for volunteers to coax the church's historic heating system back to life and to help protect the village hall during the nightmare of the Sunday School Christmas party.

Indeed, the annual Sunday School party is very much welcomed by senior members of the choir as a great opportunity to do some profitable poaching. In order that the congregation may get a little peace and quiet and have a chance of hearing what the vicar is talking about at Sunday morning service, the children of this parish are, from a very early, post-creche, age, drafted into the Sunday School into the all-embracing care of a lovely-spirited lady who still believes firmly that all children are at heart the angelic beings of Victorian children's hymns. With a clear and pure conscience she dismisses all junior vandalism and violence as merely the result of appealing high spirits.

"merely the result of appealing high spirits"

Among those pupils with the most appealing high spirits are always a clutch of potential choir recruits and regularly each year, while policing the Sunday School Christmas party, the senior choir members seek to entice specially targeted ones away from the Sunday School and into the (paid) treble section of the choir. The ploy works well. The lovely-spirited lady looks upon the enticement as a richly-deserved reward for her angelic charges and indeed a step up the ladder of sainthood, and the budding saints like the idea too, particularly the bit about being paid to come to church.

Of course, once in the choir, they soon have to come to terms with the fact that the organist is quite unlike the lovely-spirited lady and considers them all as over-indulged hooligans who are a necessary evil in the maintaining of a traditional church choir, the necessary evil being kept within decent bounds by the imposition of large fines for misconduct (musical and otherwise) which can seriously deplete and sometimes be found to have completely exhausted the whole amount of one's pay when pay day comes round.

I am a guest in the choir once a year on horse show Sunday. The one surface-rippling event in the serene pool of village life (apart from the Sunday School party) is without doubt the summer horse show. It doesn't feature in any important national show calendars and is concerned entirely with carthorses, but over the years its popularity over a considerable surrounding area has grown amazingly. True to tradition, as the carthorse all but disappeared from our streets and fields, the general public suddenly realised how much they admired, and were fascinated by, those splendid beasts and more and more spectators poured into the village each year on horse show Sunday. As horse numbers continued to decline, spectator numbers rose. Some years ago when around five thousand people turned up to see thirty horses, Oscar, who is on the horse show committee, forecast that in another five years there would be ten thousand people looking at fifteen horses and eventually they would have a hundred thousand people watching a single horse.

Happily, as the big horses made a dramatic comeback in promotional and leisure fields, Oscar's prophecy proved wrong and the show now goes from strength to strength. Oscar always arranges for the full participation of the church choir in the show and we sing drinking songs on a brewery dray and in the beer tent after Matins. Then, after the close of the show, there is a special festal Evensong when a procession of drays brings people to church where we all sing 'All things bright and beautiful' and 'Fight the good fight' and everybody is jolly and gives lots of spare change to the organ fund.

On the latest occasion of the summer horse show, however, the vicar made an unprecedented request to the organist at very short notice. He would be most grateful if - just for this year - it would be possible to substitute a new hymn for 'Fight the good fight'. He explained that the hymn in question was the absolute favourite of an elder sister of his who lived in Canada and would be making her first visit to see him in over forty years, and was keen to attend the horse show Evensong. He fully realised that normally the hymns for this service, like all others, were strictly those on the handed-down list from the last organist but one, but in the circumstances perhaps - in view of the very special circumstances...

In the vestry just before the service the organist, a tall, neat, nattily-dressed man with a knowing, crinkled face, gathered the choir around him. "He wants us to sing this new thing for his sister", he explained, handing out the music copies the vicar had supplied. "As you can see, it's one of those 'Clap hands, here comes Charlie' efforts photocopied on a bit of paper with no author and no composer - and no wonder - where you have to sing two lines three times and then shout 'Alleluia' or 'Hurray' or something".

One of our basses was regarding his hymn sheet with baffled expression. "That's the trouble, of course". he rumbled. "That's the real trouble. When you've got a man like our *last* vicar - always sticking his nose in and trying to change everything - it's a pleasure to tell him what he can do with his ideas. But when you've got a bloke like *this* one - never interferes, and always ready to stand you a pint - you can't really say no".

So we didn't say no, and even the bass spokesman thundered out the vicar's sister's favourite hymn as if he'd known and loved it from the cradle. Only his nearest colleagues heard him exclaim, as the last jolly shout echoed round the church, "Where do they dig up this rubbish?" So the vicar's sister's ecstasy on hearing her favourite 'praise song' sung in 'such a thrilling , uplifting way' was not spoiled.

After the service most of the choir and congregation moved across the road to the large field where the horse show had been held and watched huge Shire horses being fed and watered and loaded into horse boxes. The lovely-spirited Sunday school lady was there too, beaming proudly at her swarming pupils who were all exhibiting their appealing high spirits by pursuing each other between the horses' legs and examining the outsized hooves at close quarters. "Such good-tempered horses, Shires", remarked the organist at my elbow. "Still", he added hopefully, "perhaps one of them will get fed up in a minute and kick out".

He raised his voice to choir practice pitch. "Get away from those hooves!" His roar echoed round the field. The Shires stood unperturbed. The budding saints scattered. The organist smiled in grim anticipation. "I'll have most of 'em in the choir next year", he gloated.

"Well, if you can get them up to the standard of your present trebles that will be marvellous", I assured him. "I thought their singing was absolutely splendid today".

"It's amazing what you can do with a bunch of hooligans if you show them who's master", he agreed. "It's the same with the vicar".

"But the vicar's not a hooligan, surely?" I exclaimed, slightly shocked. "He always seems so polite and considerate".

"Maybe, but we still have to keep a sharp eye on him", he warned. "You see, now we've given in to him about singing his sister's hymn he'll be encouraged to start pushing other things on to us as well. I know he's got a whole book of those funny sort of new hymns. He'd love to sing some of *those* at Matins".

"But he can't sing", I said.

"He thinks he can", said the organist. "When he first came here I had no end of a job convincing him that we all felt that someone in the choir should sing the versicles for him because we were anxious that he should save his voice for the sermon. He seemed very suspicious, I can tell you".

A big bouncy choir girl who always sang with the utmost healthy vigour no matter what marks of expression the composer had indicated came up to us, leading her father's

Shire horse. She pointed to her huge charge's red rosette. "A second last year, a first this year. How about that!" she beamed. Being equally captivated, as she obviously was, with the charms of Shire horses, I found myself quite naturally talking to this one and congratulating him on his win while she told him we thought he was a very handsome clever boy. And there we stood chatting - although the horse couldn't really get a word in edgeways - until the organist tapped the choir girl on the shoulder in a businesslike way and said he hoped she'd got her solo ready for next Sunday's anthem because he didn't expect to be mucking about drumming it into her at the last minute before the service. She said she knew her solo backwards and the organist said that probably was just about how she *did* know it, and she insisted that he pat her horse to show how pleased he was that he'd won a first. A delightful pair, they meandered away across the field. The organist stood watching. "Of course, we have *them* in the choir now", he remarked meditatively.

"Who?" I asked. "Shire horses?"

"Young women", he said. "In my younger days we only had choir boys. Now it's choir girls. We've got more girls than boys now".

"Things change", I said.

His voice became warm and comfortable. "Not really", he said. "They're all hooligans. Nothing changes. No, nothing really changes, thank goodness. We're lucky with our choir".

NO VACANCIES

One of the first things that struck the new vicar when he took over at the East Anglian village church where my friend, affectionately known as 'the Orrible Organ Grinder' ('Orrible' for short), is organist and choirmaster was the smallness of the choir. Being himself quite unmusical and tone deaf, the vicar did not appear to be in the least affected by the nerve-shattering uproar that the small choir and organist inflicted on the congregation Sunday by Sunday as, in the words of the gloom-laden vicar's warden, they 'slaughtered the hymns and savaged the psalms'. It was the empty spaces in the seemingly endless Victorian choirstalls that worried and saddened the vicar and moved him to plan a recruitment drive for more volunteers to 'have a go' in the choir. He said that in England, where congregations were always reluctant to sing above a whisper, unless they were on television, the greatest encouragement for them was to see the choirstalls packed with enthusiastic, joyful singers. Such enthusiasm and joy, he said, flowed out into the congregation in a great irresistible tide and in no time at all you had everyone simply raising the roof with praise.
The vicar's warden said that if the choir got even a little bit bigger everyone would raise the roof all right, but it wouldn't be with praise. Over the years the congregation had schooled themselves to put up with the choir in a most

admirable, brave, Christian manner, but enough was enough and if the vicar started recruiting he'd be pushing the choir's luck just that bit too far and he'd have a revolution on his hands.

"puzzlement deepened into dismay"

Happily unaware of the vicar's warden's dire prophecy, the vicar blundered ahead with his 'swell the glad sound' campaign with the greatest fervour. His wife, who was a bit of an artist between running, single-handed, the seven-bedroomed eighteenth-century vicarage and making tons of chutney and jam for the Christmas bazaar, designed some delightful posters depicting heavenly-looking little choir people backed by bigger, noble-looking choir people all bawling their heads off, accompanied by a fiendishly life-like representation of the 'Orrible Organ Grinder crouching over his console with all the stops out.

With touching enthusiasm the vicar was soon plastering the posters all over the village. And thereby, quite unconsciously, he inaugurated a very popular version of the type of competition that invites you to state, in not more than a dozen words, your views on something or other. Under the huge black printed exhortation to 'Join our Choir!' someone had written on the poster in the church porch: 'No experience necessary!'

And then the competition really got under way. Rapidly-lengthening lists of similarly eye-catching remarks about the choir appeared on every available poster. In a number of cases writers returned again and again to add further flashes of literary brilliance. It was even rumoured that one or two highly respected, well-read members of the congregation had been observed inscribing their entries on posters late on dark nights, while others, who normally found it difficult to think what to say on a postcard from a holiday resort, eagerly scrawled their fulsome thoughts on the posters in the full light of day.

'Orrible and his choir who had been much disturbed when the vicar had first mooted the idea of recruiting more'cheerful people to fill up the choirstalls', were intrigued by the way things were going. The choir was a sort of small select club whose members were closely related, always did things together, and had been there for years with the same hymn book, the same services, the same organist, and the same solid opposition to any new-fangled notions a vicar might suggest. They didn't take kindly to the idea of strangers barging in to the choir and upsetting things, whether they were cheerful people or not, and, as 'Orrible pointed out to me when I arrived on a visit when the poster competition was at its height, what the vicars had got to realize was that they were merely ships that passed in the night - they stayed in a parish just long enough to change everything back to front and then moved on, whereas the choir were there all the time and couldn't be expected to take seriously the fads and fancies of someone who would be gone in a few years and followed by someone else who would alter everything again, so that no one knew what they were doing.

The new vicar, of course, soon became aware of the rude additions to the posters and wondered where he had gone wrong. Puzzlement deepened into dismay as the writings became more and more adventurous and eagerly vied with one another for most atrocious insult (and, in some cases, atrocious spelling). He called a hasty meeting of the choir and organist to assure them that, as far as he and all right-minded members of the congregation were concerned, their efforts each Sunday were highly appreciated and much enjoyed, and that he hoped they would take no notice of the unfortunate scrawlings on the posters.

'Orrible immediately sought to put the vicar's mind at ease. He said the choir couldn't care less about any number of unfortunate scrawlings and they certainly weren't going to change the habits of a lifetime. He added firmly that they didn't want any new people singing in the choir either. It had taken years to get the right balance and tone (brute force and ignorance, one poster had said), and even *one* new voice would stick out like a sore thumb and spoil the whole effect.

The vicar, despite his secret belief that by making everyone in the congregation feel wanted and important he could get them all to do just whatever he required to bring his pet plans for the parish to fruition, nevertheless sensed that he wasn't going to get round the choir with flattery, and sensibly began to rethink his tactics for eliminating the depressing gaps in the choir-stalls.

Unexpected help was at hand. During a round of visiting some of the more prominent members of the congregation, he came upon a certain large, loud, very forthright lady who dragooned the church's flower-arranging team, and indeed most other members of the congregation whom she needed for frequent cleaning, renovating and tidying duties in the church and churchyard and who constantly failed in their efforts to evade her at the back of the church after Sunday Matins.

She and the new vicar appreciated and liked each other instantly. They favoured different methods of persuasion, but each realized that the other was doing a splendid job of managing what the lady called a 'cussed awkward congregation' - first-rate when you'd got through to them, but cussed awkward to deal with. And as for the choir, the lady, like the rest of the congregation couldn't abide the thought of any enlargement, but in her case her consternation had nothing to do with singing. In fact she rather liked loud noises - she made plenty of noise herself. It generally meant that people were getting on with the job, she said. "No!" she told the vicar, "filthy, dirty, ragged jeans, that's my objection".

"Ah - er - oh dear", murmured the vicar in some puzzlement.

"You see", she explained, "the choirboys never button up their cassocks - just sling 'em on and leave 'em gaping open. Consequently, as the choir stalls are open in the front, the ghastly sight that confronts me at every service is a row of filthy, dirty, ragged jeans".

"I'll certainly speak to the choir and organist..." began the vicar.

"No good", answered the lady. "Can't do anything with that lot. No good pleading or threatening - I know! But I have a proposition, vicar". She explained that she had for some time been considering making a gift to the church in memory of her late father. What if she gave a new set of choirstalls - with panelled fronts of course - that would entirely hide the dreadful jeans? The vicar beamed and said that it would be a truly lovely gesture to give such a generous gift that would bear the name of her dear father. The lady said she didn't know about the dear father bit. He'd been a dreadful old man who persistently smoked a foul pipe in bed, voted Labour and hadn't been inside a church since her christening - but she just couldn't endure the torture of the jeans much longer and new choirstalls would save her reason.

And right in the middle of Evensong the next Sunday the vicar saw the light. The new choirstalls could also be a cure for his torture of the gaping empty places in the choir. The Victorians, catering for a huge choir, had taken up most of the chancel with stalls. The new ones needed to be only half their length. That way the choir would be bunched together in unbroken ranks - no depressing spaces. The vicar smiled and felt great satisfaction as he announced a hymn in the wrong place and the choir, regardless, bellowed forth with the anthem.

Some months later 'Orrible invited me to sing in the choir at the service of dedication on the new choirstalls. I am the one exception to their 'no outsiders' rule and I've often joined them when in the area because 'Orrible reckons my voice seems to fit in very well with their style and causes no harm at all. We had a splendid uproarious service with the choir crammed into the new shorter choirstalls singing lots of martial Victorian hymns and 'Orrible's unique version of Handel's 'And the glory of the Lord', with not a pair of offending jeans in sight. The vicar too was well on form, ecstatically thanking the flower-arranging leader for her wonderful gift in memory of her - er - dear father. He then told the congregation how important they were to the life of the church and how very much he appreciated all their supportive efforts - and was there anyone who would kindly volunteer to take over the vicarage garden as the weeds were now waist high and he hadn't been used to a garden and wasn't a very good gardener?

Finally he announced that the extra space in the chancel resulting from the removal of the old choirstalls would be beautified with displays of flowers. More volunteers were therefore needed for the increased work of the flower-arranging team. The leader would be at the back of the church at the end of the service to take names.

There was a distinct feeling of relief that things were getting back to normal, that something awkward had been nicely avoided. The vicar was naively happy, the choir cautiously mollified, the uncommitted members of the congregation still hopeful that they could avoid the attention of the flower lady at the back of the church without actually appearing to do so - and the vicar's warden looked as miserable as ever. Life was tumbling along comfortably again.

GRUMBLING IS GOOD FOR YOU

It is a regrettable fact that in some parishes the presence of the church choir is, for the most part, ignored. The choir have always been there, like the bad stained glass windows and the damp stained patches on the west wall, and the congregation have long since ceased giving them any thought or consideration.

The position is very different in a certain village church where my friend Felix (his father was a fanatical admirer of Mendelssohn and his mother was an early fan of the famous cartoon cat) is organist and choirmaster. There the choir are always in the thoughts of the congregation. They keep thinking what a relief it will be when the octogenarian bass with a voice like an enraged football hooligan eventually decides to retire, and they constantly consider with desperate hope the possibility of two or three of the teenaged choir girls getting married and raising families and not having time on Sundays to shriek through the hymns and psalms half a bar ahead of the organ and the rest of the choir.

The vicar is aware of the feelings of the congregation but he also possesses a voice like unto that of an enraged football hooligan and, further, he thinks the church is very lucky in having such attractive, keen choir girls. In fact he is only too eager to inform all who mention the choir to him - and some of those who find it unmentionable as well - that he revels in a jolly good uninhibited sing - and if there's one thing the choir are good at it's uninhibited singing.

Felix is a fervent lover of tradition. One of his best-loved and immovable traditions is that of choir practice. It takes place every Sunday morning about half an hour before Matins is due to start. As soon as a few early stragglers turn up, Felix gathers them around the vestry piano and they start to run though the music for the service. The small band dispose of the psalms and canticles in something under five minutes - Felix thumps out the chants one after the other in a sort of continuous medley and the choir members nod their heads and say they know them all, and that leaves Felix free to concentrate wholly on his favourites, the hymns. All these are also well known, being always chosen from a small collection of warlike Victorian hymns with appropriately militaristic tunes that are used throughout the year whatever the season. Nevertheless, every verse of every hymn is sung at the practice in order to warm up for the service, and as more and more choir members arrive the racket grows louder and louder until just before Matins it threatens to drown out the sound of the bells, which generally set up some splendid competition as the volume of sound from the choir grows more belligerent. The bellringers always have the final advantage, however, because they carry on after the choir have to stop in order to line up and shuffle into the chancel to start the service.

As will be realized, there is no provision for a 'quiet time' for the congregation before the service, but the vicar does compensate for this by having what he calls 'meditative silence' at the commencement of the service. This gives the choir breathing space to cough, drop books, and generally settle themselves into the choirstalls, and time for the latecomers in the congregation to clatter through the squeaking doors and greet each other in the jolly manner of customers arriving in the pub for a convivial get-together. The bellringers, having completed their duty, can also be heard clumping down the three dozen hollow stairs from the belfry, discussing what went wrong with the peal.

I am always made very welcome in the choir when I visit Felix, and the most recent occasion was on a scorching hot Sunday morning in August. As we processed back into the vestry after the service, brilliant golden sunlight was streaming through the open doorway and lightening up the dust-laden dark varnished cupboards and the faded photographs of old vicars and Victorian choir outings that lined the grey stone walls. The church is early Victorian and, I believe, a listed building. Jutting from a corner of the vestry is one of those wide oblong yellow sinks that are so shallow that they encourage water to splash all over the place as soon as you turn the tap on more than a mite - and this one is supplied by the heftiest brass tap I've ever seen that responds only to the most violent force and retaliates by thoroughly drenching the forcer. I think the combination must be listed along with the church. Anyway, it held an urgent attraction for the men of the choir on this sweltering summer morning. Their substantial crimson cassocks were discarded almost before vestry dismissal prayer was said, ties were removed and the water cascaded all over the historic threadbare carpet well beyond the boundaries of the yellow sink.

By contrast, the choir girls stood around talking, looking cool, unperturbed and very attractive in their crimson gowns and snow-white cravats. The men straggled out into the churchyard, dishevelled, red-faced and wet, and assuredly on their way to The One-Eyed Pheasant. Felix finished his voluntary - a favourite of mine that sounds as though it started life played on a steam roundabout organ - and came into the vestry with the vicar, who had finished shaking hands with the departing congregation and who now proceeded with his routine flattery of the girls about their delightful singing ("I was saying to my wife at dinner only last night how fortunate we are - how very fortunate....") Then Felix led me off to lunch and a choir girl, a dark-haired charmer who lives next door to him, walked with us. In the churchyard some of the congregation lingered in small groups. A group of three middle-aged ladies of important appearance stood near the gate in loud conversation. "*They* want the choir to sing Vivaldi and that kind of thing", informed the choir girl in a conspiratorial whisper.

"What for?" asked Felix.

"They're always on about it to my mother at the W.I.", enlarged the choir girl, "in fact, about half the congregation are - and the other half just complain that we make an awful noise".

"There's no satisfying some people", said Felix.

"They say that Vivaldi is uplifting and inspiring", said the choir girl.

"Don't they like what you sing?" I asked.

She opened her eyes wide at me and looked gorgeous. "The one in the fur cape - in the middle of August, too! - says she goes home from church every Sunday with a ramping headache because of us", she said.

We drew abreast of the conferring ladies. Felix and I

"smiled at us from a great height"

greeted them. and Fur Cape smiled at us as if from a great, frosty height. "How did you enjoy the singing this morning?" asked the choir girl enthusiastically. "Smashing, wasn't it - a real good bash, don't you think?" The lady smiled at her as from an even greater frosty height and we bowed ourselves from the presence.

"Now you've done it", admonished Felix. "Now she won't make any more raspberry jam for the organ fund".

But, of course, the lady *did* make more raspberry jam for the organ fund. She *always* made raspberry jam for the organ fund, and tons of chutney too, and every jar was eagerly snapped up at the next organ fund sale. Indeed, as usual, the sale was a roaring success with nothing left on the stalls at the end of day but a battered tin kettle, a wad of parish magazines, a lot of odd shoes and some unframed photographs of people's grandfathers in Boer War uniforms.

Immediately following the sale, the evening concluded with an old-time music hall concert put on by the choir to show their gratitude for the organ fund support, and all members of the congregation were invited. Of course, the inevitable rumours had reached Felix and members of the choir that some of the congregation were saying things like "As if we don't have enough of them on Sunday without having to put up with them on Saturday as well" and "Let's hope that the long-service bass doesn't sing 'Boots' again this year. I got quite alarmed last time when he started turning purple in the last verse".

But Felix's church is a truly united one, despite the lack of Vivaldi. On the night of the concert the village hall was crammed to the rafters. The bass did sing 'Boots' again, and this time also led the audience in rendering a roof-raising performance of 'Roll out the barrel'. And at the end of the evening the superior lady with the fur cape suddenly realized that she had not only joined in vigorously with 'Any old iron' but had bawled out "More! More!" She felt ashamed and quite elated.

Felix's delightful choir girl neighbour stood by me on the

stage watching the audience struggling out through the exit lugging their bulging bags of raspberry jam and chutney and manhandling the useless junk they had purchased to donate back to the next organ fund sale. "This'll keep them happy for a bit", she opined. "They'll say nice things to my mother about the choir for a week or two. Then they'll start grousing again and saying they want Vivaldi and not so much noise. They always do".
"Will it matter?" I asked.
She wrinkled her nose in a smile that was pure enchantment. I wondered if she would stay in the choir and grow old there, as so many of us do. "Will it matter? No", she said warmly. "We *all* grumble. We *enjoy* grumbling. It keeps us happy, doesn't it".

DEMOCRACY AND ALL THAT

The new vicar at the country church where my cousin Harry has been in the choir for fifty years is very good at getting his own way. He's very democratic about it. He calls frequent and regular consultation meetings at which all members of the congregation are urged to attend because, he points out, the running of the parish must be in the hands of the parishioners and not dictated by the views of the clergy. At the meetings everybody sits in a circle so that no one appears more prominent than anyone else and the vicar then opens the consultation by firmly stating his views in detail and at a great length. There then follows a short period in which he welcomes and applauds the views of anyone he can persuade to agree with him ("Yes, indeed! Exactly! Splendid!") and advises the large number who don't agree with him, or don't know what he's talking about, that it is their Christian duty to forego their own views for the sake of progress, unity and the common good of the church. He then neatly rounds off the proceedings with a quick grace and a cup of coffee and everybody gets off home nice and early.

Thus it was, very belatedly, that the parishioners ("You are in charge. I'm here, your vicar, to carry out your wishes") realized that they had somehow sanctioned the abandoning of a much-loved hymn book, the huge expense of replacing the church's "quite dreadful Victorian East window" with modern tinted glass ("So beautiful, restful and simple"), replaced Sunday Evensong with a Happy Christian Hour and introduced a kiddies' gnome village and goldfish pond among the listed eighteenth-century tombs in the churchyard.

And it was only when the vicar, racing ahead with reforms, announced the plan ("after a full and detailed discussion") to do away with the outmoded Victorian institution of robed choirs "cluttering up our fine mediaeval chancel" that the congregation began to be vaguely aware that there was something amiss somewhere in the democratic system.

The choir themselves were mostly seasoned veterans who, over recent years, had become thoroughly used to a succession of vicars, each of whom arrived in the parish full of enthusiasm and radical thoughts, intent on sweeping away the moribund ideas of his predecessor and dragging the church from the nineteenth century to transform it into an up-to-the-minute, relevant, meaningful body - a vital community. The snag was that the various vicars' notions of how to achieve all this differed so widely and each had stayed in the parish for such a short time before deciding that the whole place was beyond any kind of help, democratic or otherwise, that the parishioners, when they tried to envisage the new vital community, became thoroughly confused. On the other hand the choir, who never tried to envisage anything beyond what they'd always done, carried on supremely, happily unconcerned - until the vicar's latest bombshell.

On the Sunday evening after the parishioners learned that they had made the decision to remove the choir from the chancel, the choir held an emergency meeting in the back room of the Charging Bull with Cousin Harry in the chair. Normally at choir meetings the organist took the chair but on this occasion the thought of the democratic decision he had apparently helped to make had so upset him that it was felt that he was not really the best person to conduct this meeting in view of the somewhat rude, indeed violent, language he was tending to use in front of the choir girls whenever the vicar was mentioned. So, spluttering pipe clamped in a corner of his mouth, he sat at the back of the room under a violently rolling cloud of smoke, muttering awful threats.

Cousin Harry sat at a rickety card table behind a tankard of beer and attempted to field questions and suggestions here and there that he could disentangle from the boxing-ring racket of everyone shouting at once. "He says we've decided that the choir won't wear robes any more and they'll sit in with the congregation", he bawled. "He says we're one united family which we can't be with the choir stuck up the steps behind the screen". Cousin Harry was careful not actually to mention the vicar's name in view of the trouble they were having with the organist.

"Well, all that's out for a start", thundered the principal bass, a huge gentleman blocking everyone's view in the middle of the front row. He could be heard easily even at this meeting because, without really trying, he could drown out all other sounds for hundreds of yards around. That's why he was principal bass. The hubbub ceased and everyone turned in his direction. "We've always been robed. We've always been in the chancel". His clenched fist shot up dramatically in the direction of a broken light fitting that hung drunkenly from the ceiling. "That's where we belong. That's where we stay!"

"He says robed choirs in the chancel are an outmoded Victorian idea", put in an indignant little man from under the bass's arm. "He says, before that, choirs wore ordinary clothes and were hidden away in the gallery with a double bass fiddle and a flute or something".

"It'll be even worse than that now", took up a prominent-looking contralto lady with blue hair and lots of bangles. She raised a hand, pointing imperiously at Cousin Harry as the bangles clattered musically down her arm. "If he thinks I'm going to sit down in the congregation with all those people who can't sing and their kids running up and down the pews, bawling, he's got another think coming, united family or no united family".

A man who had not joined in the general fray but had been sitting quietly solving the Sunday Times crossword puzzle now spoke. He looked remarkably like Beniamino Gigli and was indeed the choir's leading tenor. "There's no immediate worry", he assured silkily. "He can't push us out that easily. He'll need a faculty to get rid of the choirstalls and that'll take ages, knowing *our* diocese."

"He won't need a faculty to get rid of *us*", countered the huge bass. "He says we're to sit down in the congregation from next Sunday. He says it's going to be a real family get-together. There's some christenings - three babies and a man of eighty-five who missed out earlier - and some jolly praise songs".

"Heaven help us", groaned Blue Hair.

"There's not much chance of that", rumbled the huge bass. "We'll have to help ourselves".

Gigli smiled and spoke smoothly. "It'll all blow over. We've had this kind of thing before. There was that vicar chap before the last one. He tried it the other way round.

He wanted the congregation to sit in the choirstalls with the choir. It's this family thing these modern clerics have got sold on. Everybody's got to be massed together and shaking hands".

"together as a family"

The smoke around the organist had by now completely enveloped him and was threatening to obscure the rest of the protesters. There was no doubt the organist was becoming very upset...

Thus far into the crisis I learned from letters from Cousin Harry, who likes to keep me in touch with the goings-on at his church, as I like to keep him in touch with the goings-on at mine. Then, as usual, came my invitation for my once-yearly visit to Cousin Harry, when traditionally I was a guest in the choir and sat next to Cousin Harry, who brought me up to date in detail with parish politics in a penetrating, hissing whisper right through both lessons and the sermon at Matins.

Apparently the vicar's dreamed-of service when everyone - congregation, choir and Gigli's cat Rossini - sat together as a family took place on the Sunday morning before my visit and the vicar's ecstasy lasted through the rest of the day and until the Monday evening, when a deputation from the parish called at the vicarage to say that, despite the importance of the family spirit, the general feeling was that the choir should stay firmly in the choirstalls. A dozen members of the congregation were afraid the choir would displace them from their favourite seats behind pillars or next to radiators, others agreed that although the principal bass's voice sounded fine and stirring from the choirstalls, it tended only to stir up trouble in the pews where it frightened the young children. Yet others objected to choir members passing round foul-smelling throat lozenges throughout the service or reading paperbacks during the sermon. So by and large the congregation felt strongly that the choir should be in the choirstalls where they'd always been and could do no harm. It seemed right and proper.

Finally a very enterprising member of the congregation, who was considered an expert on the history of the village church because, from time to time, he produced articles about it in the parish magazine which he'd copied word for word from books in the public library, discovered during his researches that the choir were not in fact "cluttering up the fine mediaeval chancel", as the vicar had alleged. The fine mediaeval chancel had apparently fallen down in the middle of the eighteenth century and the present one was a replacement built in 1887 to commemorate Queen Victoria's golden jubilee.

The vicar recognizes when he has been outmanoeuvred. He doesn't cry over spilled milk. He forges ahead regardless. Cousin Harry tells me that his latest call for a full parish meeting is to enable everyone to decide democratically that the pews should be removed and be replaced with tip-up, cinema-style seats. Alas for democracy. The parishioners have learned their lesson. Plans for a protest march to the vicarage are already under way.

LIGHTS AND LEAKS

When I was in the vicinity, I occasionally sang in the choir of a town where the dim religious light was very dim indeed owing to the proximity of an old railway viaduct which at least looked rather splendid, a new monolithic office block which didn't, and the church's shy electric lights that all seemed to be hiding at the tops of pillars and behind roof beams.

The vicar practiced the usual procedure of shaking hands with the congregation in the church porch after the Sunday services, but this vicar went further. He was frequently found to be hanging about in the porch *before* the service as well. The theory was that he was taking a mental note of arrivals so that he could check if they were still around at the end of the service. There were dark rumours that quite a number of the congregation, taking advantage of the dim religious light, regularly slipped out of the church by a side door during the singing of the hymn before his sermon.

He had often suggested to his warden, in a roundabout way of course, that perhaps a note could be kept of the alleged offenders, but the warden had been warden to a long line of vicars of all kinds from the autocratic to the 'all jolly chums together' variety, and regarded them all merely as ships that passed in the night, so he gave nothing away and deftly turned the conversation on to items like the reception arrangements for the Mayor and Corporation at the annual civic service, or the leaking chancel roof over the back row of the choir.

In fact, the leaking roof over the back row of the choir had been a problem for quite a number of years. No one seemed able to repair the area permanently. A succession of members of the congregation - a schoolteacher, a bus driver, an operatic tenor and a library assistant - doing a voluntary stewardship job for the church on their days off, had clambered on to the roof with slates and rolls of stuff and large tins of sticky liquid and all had been well for a month or two, and then the whole thing started again. By this time the vicar dreaded to hear of anything remotely connected with the leaking roof over the back row of the choir - indeed, he dreaded to hear of anything to do with the choir at all. Apart from the fact that they steadfastly refused to sing his kind of music and, as a body on the church council, always blocked his dearest wishes to level off the graveyard and stand all the headstones in a nice, neat, tidy line along the path to the church door, and to introduce a lily pond and a picnic area, he didn't trust the choir. For a long time he had had his suspicions that here too quite a number of them regularly evaded his sermons although, unlike the congregation backsliders, they didn't actually leave the building but simply retired to the vestry to read their Sunday papers and then returned to their places for the final hymn. The trouble was that during the sermon the vicar couldn't see the choir from the pulpit and this enhanced his suspicions of them because he had always believed that keeping a constant eye on the choir was a very important part of conducting a trouble-free service.

A contributing difficulty for the vicar, particularly at Evensong on dark winter evenings, was the custom of putting out most of the lights for the sermon except for a spotlight over the pulpit. All he could see from his bright, exalted position were pale blurs of what he took to be upturned interested faces but which he sometimes realized to his chagrin could equally be the tops of heads as they drooped in sleep. He had given the matter much thought and had tried a number of ruses in order to hold the attention of the pale blurs. Once he started his sermon by singing a verse of a comic song instead of quoting a text, and another time he opened by announcing "It's simply bucketing down outside, so you'll all be far better off in here listening to me" - and smiled to show he was only joking, but on both occasions he had the distinct impression that some of the pale blurs had then disappeared altogether.

In his early days in the parish he had, of course, more than once suggested the obvious - that the lights should be left on during the sermon, but here he had met what he finally realized was the original immovable object. Within living memory the lights had *always* been put out for the sermon. The current man whose job it was to switch them off had done so for over thirty years, except when he had been on holiday. Then the operation had been faithfully carried out by his friend, who was universally regarded as his natural successor and who, for the last twenty-five years,had firmly closed the prison-like West door of the church immediately the service started, thus obliging all latecomers to advertise their failings by forcing it open against loudly-protesting hinges.

On the occasion of one of my recent visits to the choir, the latest attempt to stem the leaking from the roof over the back row of the choir was well under way and had reached the stage where the entire set of choirstalls opposite the organ had been blanketed with fallen plaster and splintered laths. A belatedly-placed piece of protective plastic sheeting that appeared to cover only one end of one stall had collected rainwater from last night's downpour, which had eventually overflowed on to the plaster to produce an evil-looking grey fluid. This, the choirboy distributing the music for Matins had tramped into an intricate pattern all over the chancel floor.

"tramped into an intricate pattern all over the chancel floor"

As the time of the service approached the organist, an elegant middle-aged character wearing a silk gown and a cynical expression, who had been inspecting the plastered choirstalls and kept on muttering "Disgusting" and "Morons", called the choir together and told us we'd have to sit on one side of the choirstalls so there'd be rather a crush, in fact thered be an almighty crush, but we'd all have to sort ourselves out as best we could, as usual. A man standing next to me confided that it was always particularly awkward for him when we all had to sit together on one side while they were mending the roof because he found the atmosphere very claustrophobic, and if there was one time when he couldn't sing, it was when he was claustrophobic. He told me this very loudly (he was a very loud bass) and a large contralto lady floating at my other side said she *never* felt claustrophobic in crowds. In fact she adored crowds, and always loved going to football matches and winter sales. My claustrophobic colleague seemed a mite put out by this and I think he would have said more had not the vicar at that moment sped into the vestry, bellowed "Good morning!" and the vestry prayer all in one breath and hustled us before him into the church. We all made quickly for the limited accommodation in the mainly unobstructed choirstalls on one side, but had to mill around in a rather undignified manner while a soprano lady with a minute lace handkerchief attempted to remove some outlying plaster dust from the large space she had grabbed. Eventually I found myself sitting at the end of a stall balancing on two retired hassocks that were bursting at the seams and had been hastily brought from the vestry where they normally supported a three-legged cupboard full of music, forgotten umbrellas and empty wine bottles.

However, I was suddenly aware of the presence, threatening to envelope me, of the contralto lady who adored crowds. Equally, she didn't adore people like me who drifted into the choir at odd times and took up valuable space. With a smart tap or two on the back of my neck from her outsized handbag, she indicated that she had no seat, and not wanting to offer her such a basic one as mine I slipped back into the vestry in the slender hope of finding an overlooked chair or some less disreputable hassocks. I was unsuccessful, of course, and returned to find the lady firmly in possession of my hassocks so, with no other choice, I made myself scarce sitting on a most uncomfortable eighteenth century tomb, which had-been cavalierly blocked off by the Victorian choirstalls, where I stayed throughout the service. I don't know what the sermon was about because I couldn't hear it from my position, but I did find some fascinating reading in the epitaph which crammed itself all over the front and halfway down one side of the tomb.

Apparently the occupant had been an undeniably perfect human being - a peerless paragon of a fellow - pious, generous and loyal, blameless, gentle and charitable, kind to his wife, children, servants and passing vagrants, and always full of pity for those who hadn't managed to get themselves so well off as he had. He was constantly only to eager to forgive villains and set them on a righteous path after first being only too eager to dole out the most generous sentences of cleansing chastisement to them as the local JP. As brave as a lion, he had blundered, uninvited, into all kinds of heathen parts all over the world and had fearlessly slaughtered untold numbers of wild beasts and was loved and respected by all - except, presumably, the wild beasts.

Although on this occasion the usual members of the congregation doubtless escaped before the sermon, I am pretty certain that no one from the choir got out. At the end of the service I was able to stroll freely from the paragon's tomb, but the people in the choirstalls took quite a time to disentangle themselves and circumnavigate the soprano with the lace handkerchief, who still seemed to be keen on dusting her seat, and the crowd-loving contralto, who had already gathered around her an audience of the less strongminded choir members in order to form a subcommittee to register yet another complaint about the leak situation...

I came upon the church again some months later on a wet Monday afternoon, and by chance found the vicar sorting some papers in his stall in the chancel. I asked him how things were going and received a most enthusiastic reply. He pointed to various parts of the church. "How about that!" he said. "Brand new lighting system throughout. Only been in a month". He obviously noted my look of surprise. "Yes, cost quite a packet", he beamed. "But things have been happening around here, I can tell you. We've got a new treasurer - young, very keen type - into everything. Went through the books with a fine toothcomb. Unearthed some sort of church fund going back to the eighteenth century. Seems to have been forgotten and hidden for years". He pointed to my late uncomfortable seat, the paragon's tomb. "Matter of fact, it appears *he* started it for providing church candles. Anyway, we used it for the lights and they're the very latest. You can dim them, like theatre and cinema lights. Our man who sees to the lights -"

"Puts them out for the sermon", I dared.
He grinned. "Well, he's absolutely *fascinated* and, of course, we only *dim* them for the sermon now. I can see everyone quite clearly". His eyes twinkled. "So much *nicer*, I find".
"And what about the leak over the choirstalls?" I ventured.
He looked up to the chancel ceiling with the calm confidence vicars are supposed to have. "I trust, you know, I trust", he intoned.
I looked up also. A large drop of dirty water hit me squarely between the eyes.

STRANGE GOINGS-ON

On my latest visit to my cousin Jack, who lives in a delightfully secret hideaway on the outskirts of a South of England country town, I was most impressed and encouraged to note that the choir of the local church where he is organist and choirmaster had nearly doubled in size since I'd last joined them a few months previously. After choral Matins on a golden, serene Sunday in June, we sat in the churchyard and Jack explained a few points to me.

"There are some very strange goings-on these days in one or two churches around here", he informed me darkly. "It was only when *their* choir people started turning up here and asking to join *our* choir that we found out".

"Goings-on?" I prompted.

"Goings-on indeed", he confirmed. "It's all to do with new vicars".

"Of course", I agreed.

Apparently the new vicar of one of the churches concerned was one of those who see it as their mission to break into the entertainment business by turning their churches into a sort of variety theatre-cum-concert hall and sports centre with a small area tucked away in the vestry for the use of the persistently unprogressive minority who still expect to attend a church service on Sunday instead of taking part in a vital Christian quiz or watching a meaningful, thought-provoking, multi-church review. Jack reckons that as soon as one of these show-biz clergy gets his way in a parish the first thing to be made redundant is the choir, because it's just not considered at all progressive, vital or meaningful for congregations to stand about in pews listening to a choir chanting four-square psalms and singing hymns full of old-fashioned words.

The unfortunate choir in this case had not officially been made redundant but members felt themselves to be such back numbers that they might as well not be there at all. "So they looked around for a safe berth and thought of us", explained Jack. And soon other refugees started turning up from another nearby church that also had a new vicar. Here, according to Jack, a great shake-up of the services had taken place, as a result of which prayers and 'praise songs' on bits of paper and cards and gaily-coloured leaflets had taken the place of the prayer and hymn books, and groups with guitars and drums had ousted the choir and organ. Pews had been ripped out and yellow plastic cafe-style chairs substituted, and the congregation were supposed to stamp and clap while they sang, and everybody had to keep on smiling and shaking hands.

Now the vicar of Jack's church is what Jack calls a proper clergyman. He conducts services in the traditional manner, dresses so that you can see he *is* a clergyman and, luckily for the choir, has no plans for moving on, retiring, or turning his church into a leisure centre, so the choir feel pretty safe at the moment. The new members are, however, a mixed blessing. The fact is that until the recent immigration of singers, all the members of Jack's choir belonged to one of three families who between them had provided the choir for about two hundred years. Jack says that in situations like this you have to be very careful about letting in outsiders, but on the other hand one shouldn't look gift horses in the mouth, and anyway the extra members will be very useful during the summer months when, in strict rotation, each of the three founder families goes on holiday en bloc, thus at a stroke reducing the choir by a third.

As a relative of Jack's I'm accepted in the choir as family whenever I'm in the vicinity on a Sunday. I always enjoy myself and my latest visit was no exception. During choral Evensong I sat next to one of the newly arrived refugees, a man who had been a sergeant-major and a town-crier, who kept on clearing his throat very determinedly and took no notice whatsoever of the marks of expression -or, for that matter, some of the actual notes - in his music but bellowed forth with gladsome voice and great enthusiasm. I could see he'd got the idea all right and was settling down nicely in the traditional ways of our choir. He would be no trouble.

I wasn't so sure about others of the new recruits. One was a tall thin man of uncertain age and voice who sang half a bar behind everyone else and during the anthem vigorously polished his glasses every time he missed a lead or came in at the wrong place. And directly in front of me in the soprano line was another new member, a middle-aged lady of spare appearance and darting steely eyes who, I feel, will have to mend her ways if she means to stay with us. While we were singing she kept up a loud sighing and tut-tutting and looked very cross indeed. And during the sermon she seemed to be pointing out things in the music in the most forceful manner to the choir girl next to her, who had just offered her a surreptitious liquorice allsort.

"and looked very cross indeed"

The choir girl, a member of a founder family, appeared most puzzled by the new recruit's violent attitude, particularly as she (the choir girl) couldn't read music and hadn't the faintest idea what the lady was hissing about. After the service, the tall uncertain recruit continued to polish his glasses very enthusiastically and announced that he'd enjoyed every minute of the singing. He reckoned that the choir had, perhaps, rather raced ahead of him a bit in one or two places - it was the kind of thing he'd noticed in other choirs where he'd sung - but he was sure that they would sort out that little difficulty in time.

The cross lady soprano recruit, on the other hand, continued to be very cross indeed. As she placed her choir gown in a protective plastic cover and hung it as far as possible from all the other gowns and cassocks which were suspended in a grubby jumble at the end of a tarnished brass rail, she was heard to remark to no one in particular that in the - although she said in herself - very professional City of London church choir of which she had been a member before moving to the country, all singers had passed stiff auditions and were not the sort of people who couldn't read music and were in the habit of passing round liquorice allsorts during the sermon. She'd have to consider very carefully whether she could, after all, continue to lend her services to Jack's choir. One could not expect *too* much from amateurs, but there was a limit...

And it was during this time of uncertainty that another complicated situation arose. The new local mayor, who had nor been to church for years except for civic services and important weddings and funerals ("Love to come, I"m sure - many of my best friends are churchgoers - oh, yes - but you know how it is - the business and the council work - just no time"), had been giving thought to his forthcoming first civic service as mayor, and had suggested that instead of involving merely the parish church, as was the former custom, *all* the churches in the area should be involved in "a really great get-together" of the congregations and choirs. "After all", he had told the local press, "we all belong to one beautiful part of the country, one -" (he was about to say what he was always yearning for, "one all-embracing party", but realized in the nick of time that this would definitely not go down well at the town hall with the opposition party) "one happy, helping community", he finished, using the phrase he had thought up quite unaided and had used with no little pride at countless party functions.

As soon as the mayor's view was made known, the parish church organist, an old friend of Jack's and, like him, a last ditch traditionalist phoned Jack. "Can you imagine the kind of service they'll have to come up with to suit us and the do-it-yourself clappers and stampers?" he asked. Jack agreed that the mind boggled and reckoned that in particular the mayor and corporation in their robes and funny hats would have an awful job performing the activity bits.

"If it had been in the days when we all had the same prayer book and hymn books and you could walk into any church in the country and know what you'd be getting, the civic service would be easier to arrange", said Jack.

"You knew the stuff word for word", agreed the parish church organist, "note for note, year after year. You could do it with your eyes shut. In fact, the mayor and corporation usually *did* have their eyes shut".

"Particularly in the sermon", said Jack.

"Those were the days. You knew where you were", said the parish church organist.

"You *wonder* where you are now", said Jack.

"I suppose they'll have some kind of rehearsal for the service", speculated the parish church organist. "Ah! Just think of it!"

Jack just thought of it - his choir and the parish church choir, the pop groups and the stampers and clappers, the professional soprano who didn't like liquorice allsorts being handed round, the man who had trouble with people always singing ahead of him, the mayor whose best friends were churchgoers, the 'real' vicars, the 'show-biz' vicars, the Book of Common Prayer, Hymns A and M - not to mention the Matins congregation at Jack's church who never went to any other service and would raise Cain if Matins were cancelled for the civic service.

"See you at the rehearsal. Just think of it!" gloated the parish church organist.

SUPPORTING CAST

The choir of the village church where my Great Aunt Agatha holds sway is the biggest for miles and miles. Every Sunday the flamboyant Victorian choir stalls are overflowing with choir members of all ages, arrayed in superbly tailored cassocks of richest wine red with immaculately laundered linen surplices.

The new vicar is entirely responsible for this splendid turnout. During the first few Sundays of his ministry in the parish, his great sense of occasion was sadly shattered when he found himself conducting services amid the lonely expanse of empty dusty choirstalls, the last surviving choir member, a venerated figure who, as a boy, had sung at a service commemorating Queen Victoria's Diamond Jubilee, having recently retired. The vicar immediately set to work employing his considerable charm and powers of persuasion, which included downright barefaced flattery, to recruit an entire new choir, and nowadays, as he never tires of proclaiming, his great joy is to be "up there in the chancel, backed by my great company of harmonious support".

The only trouble is that only four people in the great company can sing or read music and as, for various reasons, these - a soprano, contralto, tenor and bass - cannot be present together for many services during the year, the choir can seldom rise above the limits of a handful of those modern hymns that are presumably intended to be bawled in a sort of football-crowd unison and are indeed enthusiastically led by the vicar, who is very keen on football and who, according to the organist, has a sort of modified football hooligan's voice.

Great Aunt Agatha, without whose approval and blessing little can take place in the church, fell instant victim to the vicar's machinations, like almost everyone else in the parish ("I simply cannot believe that you were a landgirl forewoman in the Second World War, Agatha. They just didn't allow babes in arms to join the Land Army") and was one of the first to join the new choir where, within a week or two, she had elected herself choir secretary and drawn up a set of rules to be strictly observed by all members. Great Aunt Agatha knowing nothing whatsoever about music and being tone deaf, these didn't directly concern music but dealt with items like punctuality, the wearing of suitable footwear to accompany the wine coloured cassocks (no filthy trainers, rubber boots or high-heeled shoes with sequins), not chewing, whispering or snoring during the sermon, and the absolute necessity for the gentlemen of the choir not to exit from the vestry after Sunday Evensong in the manner of a cattle stampede and thus give the impression that they were trying to beat the gentlemen of the congregation to the pub.

The organist, a competent player, although he much preferred the sound of a brass band going at full blast and, in fact, played first trombone in the local band, had played the organ for so long to empty choirstalls that he completely ignored the presence of the new choir. Indeed, it was generally believed that he didn't even know they were there. He had his own private entrance to the organ loft and, once in his one-man haven, he sat facing his two manuals and became completely engrossed in playing everything in the manner of a giant brass band thundering out a Sousa march. Even during the intervals between the hymns, he was never seen to turn and look down at the choir, but sat seemingly mesmerized by the sight of dozens of photos of steam locomotives that were pinned and stuck all over the non-playing parts of the organ. He revered steam locomotives. Between performing in the brass band and on the organ, his great delight was to take turns in driving or stoking an ancient tank engine pulling parties of riotous school children and older enthusiasts with woolly hats and cameras along a three mile stretch of line that British Rail had got rid of in the process of 'streamlining the local service'.

Not that the organist was an unfriendly man. Some of the choir members also helped out with the tank engine and had fine times with him in their happy world of steam and nostalgia, but the new choir was never mentioned.

The first time I visited Great Aunt Agatha after the forming of the choir, she invited me to join them for Sunday morning service but warned me not to sing in my normal alto voice because, she said, it wasn't natural and wouldn't fit in and would put everyone off. She said I was to sing the vicar's splendid relevant vital new-age hymns in a manly voice with bags of enthusiasm and spirit, with a smile on my face and joy in my heart. Did I understand? I assured her that I'd got the idea and reckoned I could manage the manly voice all right, but I wasn't so sure about the joyful, heartfelt smile because most earlier encounters I'd had with both the words and music of splendid relevant vital new-age hymns had tended to put me into a very bad temper. Anyway, Great Aunt Agatha took me into the choir vestry and, elbowing her way through a mass of people putting on wine-red cassocks, deposited me with a ruddy, sturdy choirboy with a large round gleeful face, who she directed to brush his awful hair and then to fit me up with a suitable cassock and surplice. The ruddy lad combed his hair back

"combed his hair back with his fingers"

with his fingers and, after the briefest inspection of my person, produced with obvious pride one of the new cassocks, which fitted me perfectly. Adding a snowy white surplice, he asked me if I was used to singing in a choir where I came from, because if I wasn't it didn't matter at all. Take him, for example. He'd never sung in a choir before, in fact he'd never sung at all since he'd been told off about it at school. But the new vicar reckoned you could do anything if you sort of kept on with it. And he was right. "And now I'm in the choir" he ended, not without a modest satisfaction.

I said I did sing in a choir and I knew what he meant. "And how about your organist?" I asked. "How do you get on with him?"

"Who?" he said.

"Your organist", I repeated.

"Oh, he's still here", he confirmed. "I think he's been here for years and years. But we don't see him much. He's up in the organ loft, you see". He suddenly beamed. "Well, we *do* see him. Sometimes he drives this steam train. It's a jolly good train. We all go on it and it blows soot all over people's washing, and they get real mad. It's jolly good fun".

"I thought he might take choir practice", I said.

"Choir practice?" he queried. "We don't have that".

"No practice?"

"Well", he amended, "sometimes just before the service the vicar says he's got another new hymn and he tralas it to us and then we all trala it back, and it goes all right in the service".

"That's amazing", I said. He seemed reluctant to accept the implied compliment.

"Well, not really", he said. "All the vicar's new hymns are the same, actually. When you've sung one, you've sung 'em all".

And as it happened, this was one of those times when the vicar fancied another new hymn. A tall figure, whose middle-aged good looks were enhanced by what Great Aunt Agatha referred to as a 'very classy' silk cassock, he made an impressive entry into the vestry, taking centre stage in front of a huge sepia photograph of a Victorian vicar of the parish who had glared down at everyone for over a hundred years. The new vicar surveyed his supporting cast with pride. "Something very special this morning", he announced. "We'll all enjoy singing *this*". He distributed to eager hands sheets of pink notepaper on which appeared groups of blurred typed words and, for some reason, a drawing of what looked like a lopsided combine harvester. "Thanks for the fruits of the earth", he enlightened. "Tune written by a friend of mine who does this kind of thing so well. Goes like this". He thumped the top of the never-used vestry piano and bellowed a cheerful noise for a few seconds, and then we all joined in and trala-ed when we couldn't read the words, and the vicar said fine, fine, that would be fine, and we all moved into church in a dignified procession while the organist amused himself with some mighty Wagnerian strains from the Twilight of the Gods.

The vicar got on with the service - a colourful mixture of Matins, community hymn singing and whatever came into his head on the spur of the moment - very briskly and I found that I could indeed sing all the hymns straight of as if I'd known them for years. It was only a question of keeping count of the number of times you repeated each line, and there you were. I did at one point repeat a line once too often, but most of the choir did, here and there, and no great harm was done to the overall effect as long as everyone kept on looking joyful.

At the end of the service the vicar paid his usual compliment to the outstanding support of the choir, and we all processed out into the vestry feeling wanted and appreciated. And the man next to me, who was still humming the tune of the last hymn, said there was no doubt about it - a good choir was *most* important for waking up the congregation on Sunday mornings. We left the church together and, as we drew abreast of a small door half hidden by rampant hollyhocks and two dustbins overflowing the dead flowers behind the vestry, the organist emerged carrying a bulging, battered music case and a shovel. "He's doing stoking duty on the engine this afternoon", explained my colleague. "Why not come along and meet him?"

I too am fascinated by steam power. I eagerly accepted his invitation and later that afternoon found myself in an adoring group of steam buffs gazing at a small gleaming tank engine, lovingly restored, no doubt by devoted weekend workers. Shovelling with a will and a shiny, coal dust-streaked face, the organist was a happy man. During a pause in his labours my choir colleague introduced me. We talked about steam engines, of course, but quite how we later got onto the topic of church choirs I'm not sure. "I've been thinking of trying to start a choir again at the church", the organist said. "We've got some good voices here in the engine shed. We do quite a bit of barbershop singing in our spare time".

"But -" I began.

"We really do *need* a choir", he went on. "It appears that this new vicar of ours thinks so too. Now and again lately he seems to have even raked up one or two visiting choirs. Goodness knows where he gets 'em from. None of 'em can sing a note - dead useless, all of them , if you ask me". he wrinkled his brow and took up his shovel again. "Strange thing about them too - they all seem to wear the same kind of funny red cassocks".